Jevon and the Mango Tree

Jacqueline Wray-Johnson

illustrated by Phillip J. Robinson

© 2018 Jacqueline Wray-Johnson
All rights reserved.

ISBN: 1979811423
ISBN-13: 9781979811422
Published by Amazon

J. Daniel this is for you.

Shanell, Gabriella, Abigail, Lovell and Jaeden; continue to dream big!

Kaneen, thanks for designing my cover, your input made it possible.

I can't wait until I get to Jamaica to climb trees, Jevon thought as he sat in the airplane. He was growing impatient, reminiscing on the stories his mother had told of the big, open land where they could run and play.

Jevon hoped there would be fruit trees for him to climb. If only he could climb.

That was the problem. He needed to learn but thought that would be a silly question to ask, so he hadn't bothered asking anyone.

Mr. and Mrs. Philkips were returning to a quaint little district in Browns Town after living in Britain for more than ten years. They wanted their children to get a taste of what life was like growing up in the Caribbean. This way, the couple hoped, their family would truly understand what their life had been like back then.

Jevon had been only two years old when his parents migrated to the United Kingdom. Growing up in the United Kingdom was all he knew.

High-rise buildings surrounded the three-bedroom maisonette on the third floor of a block of flats that he lived in. There was an abundance of shops and shortage of open land.

Jevon lived with his father, Seymour; his mother, Ruby; three sisters, Shanell, Kaneen, and Gabriella; and his youngest brother, Josiah.

They lived in an area called Tufnell Park in North West London. It was a lovely neighborhood near the popular tourist area Camden Town. It took about five minutes to walk to the nearest underground station. Buses were readily available on his doorstep. Within minutes he could be in the hustle and bustle of the famous Oxford Street. Yet the family never felt like it was their home.

City life had become a burden for his parents, and the decision to return home to Jamaica was imminent. His mother always bragged about feeling the lovely fresh air against her skin and listening to the chirping of the birds each morning. She was simply tired of the pollution in London.

The look of admiration she had on her face when she talked about eating foods from her own garden was like when a person finds a treasure chest of gold. This excitement of home emanating from his mother when she talked about her birthplace captivated Jevon's heart. He wanted to explore for himself. He couldn't wait to leave. He was eager to experience all that his mother so carefully described.

So interesting were the stories that Jevon thought it must be an adventure to live in paradise (the name his father used to describe Jamaica). "It was nothing short of living a dream, son," his father had said, looking in the distance as he sat on the balcony of the flat. Even though he'd been looking at the Arsenal Stadium and the BT Tower in the distance, it was as if he were looking at the beautiful Caribbean Sea with the orange sun setting on the edge.

The family was into a lot of physical activities and took early-morning runs in the nearby park or just strolled around, taking in the scenery. Parliament Hill was a large park with duck ponds and a playground. Jevon's family often went to the area, but it didn't provide the same joy his mother spoke about.

"When you climb trees as a child and pick your own fruits—either guava, sweet sop, and oh, the mango is a treasure—you feel a sense of independence like none other." These were his mother's words, but she had said them so often they were cemented in his brain.

As the airplane landed at Donald Sangster's International Airport in Montego Bay, Jevon said, "Oh, Mom, I can already feel the difference in the air."

"Oh really?" she asked as if she couldn't believe he did.

"Yes, I do. I don't feel as if it's choking me. I just feel so, so…" He paused, searching for the correct word to say, with the hope, of course, of impressing his mother. "Refreshed."

The smile of approval hit her face immediately. "Come here, my son," she said and planted a kiss on his cheek.

No one paid much attention to the journey home. They were much too eager to see the house.

Acres Green Heights certainly lived up to Jevon's mother's descriptions. A variety of trees layered the sides of the road. The warm but cool air made him feel sleepy. The mountainous terrain offered wavering hills and valleys. Red and yellow hibiscus beautifully decorated the landscape. The crotons formed a uniform fence around the perimeter of each plot. Yellow, red, pink—they were a mix of various colors all carefully trimmed and cut into intricate designs. Houses like mini-mansions sat comfortably on the land. They looked spacious. The land around them was surprisingly very big—unlike the massive blocks of flats that the family were accustomed to seeing squeezed onto a small plot of land.

As they approach the large entrance lined with beautiful croton, their house sat so peacefully on a large plot of land with manicured lawn that blanketed the whole plot. It provided a welcoming sight as if to embrace the family and tell them 'welcome home'.

The blue painted wooden house seemed old but there was an admirable beauty about it. The paint peeled from some areas of the outside wall, leaving a new color formed from the heat of the sun and constant beat of the rain drops. The usually shiny aluminum zinc roof had a bronze color which shows that it had been there for some years. Structurally it seemed sound and even though there were a few signs of wears and tears here and there, the family loved it. It was home, and that was all that mattered to them.

Living in Jamaica was something Jevon's parents had talked about for years. Now they were finally going to live in the tropics. Jevon was excited. His mother had always talked about growing up and being able to pick guava, pawpaws, and pears off the fruit trees in her yard.

This fascinated Jevon so much that as soon as he arrived at the house in Acres Green Heights, he scoped out the yard for possible fruit trees. He was not disappointed. In fact, there was quite a variety to choose from. Trees ranged from coconut, mango, naseberry, sweet sop, soursop, ackee, pear—which was called avocado—and cherry.

The big mango tree in the front yard instantly amazed him.

How to climb trees was a mystery to him, but when his parents bought a house with more than twelve fruit trees on the property, solving the mystery became a possibility. Tufnell Park had no fruit trees for him to climb, and here he was with a good variety of trees to choose from.

One day while Jevon was at school, his dad picked some mangos. When he came home, he was given one. The rich, succulent juices poured out on his T-shirt as he bit into the mango, enjoying its delicious taste. The fragrance, too, was exceptional. The mango was so soft against his teeth he reached the seed much too soon, disappointed the meal had ended.

Immediately, he went by the mango tree and spoke to it. "I must get some more of those juicy Julie mangos up there." *The only problem is how I am going to get them*, he thought. *I must climb this tree!*

The Julie mango tree was quite a big tree. It seemed to be as old as the house.

The branches spread widely in almost every direction. Its trunk had a diameter of about twenty-five centimeters. The extended branches formed a round bench in the center. To get to the mangos, which were perched at the peak of the branches, Jevon most definitely had to climb the tree. Reaching with a long stick would damage the mango, as it would smash upon hitting the ground. Jevon wondered how his father had gotten the mango off the tree.

He must have climbed it, he thought.

His friends at school bragged how they could climb, so it was embarrassing for a boy his age not to be able to climb a tree. If his friends ever found out that he couldn't climb, he wouldn't be able to return to school. He would not be able to endure the teasing and mocking that they were capable of. So, he started planning how he would climb the mango tree.

Early one Saturday morning, before anyone in his household had awakened, Jevon quietly sneaked out of the house and ran down to the Julie mango tree. He had his sandals on and kept them on, as the trunk of the tree seemed rough.

He held on to the tree as if he were hugging it and attempted to push himself up as if he were climbing. As he lifted his feet, one after the other, onto the trunk, he couldn't go up, no matter how hard he tried.

He tried for over an hour until he started talking to the tree. "Come on, Julie tree, how did my dad climb you to get the mango?"

Well, this is no fairy tale, so the tree gave him no response.

He stood back, and a thought came to him. He ran, then jumped onto the trunk while trying to get a good grip with his sandals on. Sadly, he lost his grip and came sliding down.

He did not realize how much time had elapsed since he'd first come outside. His sisters were now out playing. He quickly ran from the tree in an attempt not to be noticed.

A month passed, and how to climb a tree was no longer a mystery Jevon needed to solve. It was now a matter of desperation.

He received a school assignment to research the national heroes of Jamaica. As he was on the Internet, he took this opportunity to find out how to climb a tree. He typed "how to climb a tree," and Google gave him about five million results. He was shocked, so much information existed about climbing trees.

He clicked on the first website listed on the front page of the results. He didn't have much time to read. So, he quickly scanned through their information.

He went on over five different web pages, and none of them gave any detailed explanation of the techniques of climbing a tree. He was disappointed but still hopeful. One website stated, "It is not impossible to climb a tree, but it takes lots of muscle power and concentration." He looked at his hands and wondered if he had enough muscle to give him the power he needed. Another website informed him that climbing a tree was a fun and exciting childhood pastime. It further stated that it would be a challenge but a great experience.

Jevon was hopeful. A challenge but a great experience. A challenge but a *great* experience. The more he repeated the word, the more eager he was to climb.

Nothing could deter him now.

No challenge would hinder him.

One Saturday morning, Jevon woke up quite early. This was the day he would climb the Julie mango tree. Dad had gone to work and would be away for most of the day. Mom was busy tidying the house, cooking, and keeping tabs on the two smaller children. So, he was ready to implement his climbing ideas.

Jevon took the ladder from the garage. The ladder was about fifteen feet long. He used all his strength to pull it up against the coconut tree. Because of the layout of the mango tree's trunk, the ladder could not lean against it. He needed a straight edge, and the coconut tree provided that. To his surprise the ladder reached almost three-quarters of the height of the tree. With a massive smile on his face and a bubble of joy in his belly, Jevon climbed the ladder. He was so overjoyed with his efforts that he forgot his fear of heights.

Only when he saw his two-year-old brother, Josiah, riding down the driveway on his scooter did he realize how high he was. By this time, he had already climbed about eighteen of the twenty rungs on the ladder.

His heart pounded so hard and loud that he thought it would jerk him off the ladder. The ground seemed to be so far away that he felt as though he would break in pieces if he fell.

However, he remembered his mother always took a deep breath when she was upset about something. So, he took a deep breath and returned to the task—the important task at hand. He was climbing while thinking and was surprised to see that he had only two rungs left to climb. He braved the odds and quickly went up the two remaining rungs.

Wow! He felt good. The experience was exhilarating!

He could see the big jelly coconuts at the top of the tree. If he could just grip the trunk and climb, so proud of himself would he be.

Of course, having reached so far, there was no way he was going down unless he attempted to climb. So, he prayed his actions would be a success.

With that in mind, he placed both legs and arms around the tree and pushed himself up.

He leaned over as far as he could to catch any nearby branch of the mango tree.

His sandals were so slippery he gripped with his thighs instead. For a moment, he felt like a jockey. He lifted his body and tried to push himself up. This movement caused him to reach about three feet from the top of the ladder.

Suddenly, he started sliding off the coconut tree. He was sliding so fast that he thought he was on a roller coaster. His T-shirt was pulled from under his belly. With his belly rubbing against the trunk, being scraped, turning bright red, he didn't have time to think of how to react to this sudden happening. His hand was sore, and his thighs felt as if they had been smashed.

Jevon dared not look down. He closed his eyes and prayed for even one of his feet to hit the top rung of the ladder. This way he would be able to climb down. His prayer was not answered though. His body was moving so fast that it pushed the ladder out of the way, and the ladder dropped.

Jevon was now flying down the coconut tree, feet first. His belly felt hot from the scrapings of the trunk; his hands burned with heat from the bruises. His jean shorts took most of the pain from his thighs rubbing against the trunk.

He closed his eyes even tighter and held on for dear life, hoping that this roller-coaster ride would end.

Within a flash, what felt like forever for him ended. He landed on his bottom. Although his shirt was torn, skin bruised, heart pounding from the shocking event, he felt wonderful.

The ride down had been rough. Painful, yes, but Jevon felt he had achieved something. If the boys at school were to ever tease him about him not being able to climb a tree, he would ask which of them could slide down a coconut tree at a speed of twenty miles per hour without climbing from the bottom (the ladder of course being the secret.)

Oblivious to the other activities around the house, Jevon was unaware that Josiah had gone to tell his mother and sisters that Jevon was on the coconut tree. They all had watched in amazement and fear as he flew down the coconut tree.

"Boy, are you crazy!" his mother shouted. "Do you know you could seriously injure yourself?"

Before Jevon could respond, she continued. "What in the world are you trying to do, kill yourself?"

His smile quickly vanished from his face as she interrupted his thoughts of bragging to his friends.

"From now on, don't ever let me catch you near that coconut tree. You hear me, boy?"

"Yes, Mum, but, but—" Jevon stuttered.

"Yes, Mum, but what?" she stared at him with her eyes peeled.

"No! Mummy, no. I was only trying to find out how to climb the mango tree," Jevon timidly responded.

"But you weren't *on* the mango tree. I saw you on the coconut tree," his mother noted.

He explained his dilemma about the ladder being too tall for the Julie mango tree.

"Jevon, you can't climb a tree with sandals on. You have to climb the tree barefoot!"

Barefoot! What an amazing discovery! No shoes, no sandals, just plain barefoot.

It was shocking to know that his mother knew about climbing trees. Since Dad wasn't home, he thought he'd ask her to watch him try.

Ruby was taken aback that the boy would go to such lengths to climb a tree. But since there had been no trees in London for him to climb, she had to help him.

Jevon was beyond himself with excitement.

His mother instructed that he should first place his toes against the trunk as if to anchor himself, then push his body up while his feet were firmly in place. Once he managed that, he should grab the branches of the tree with his hands, gripping any lower branch, and continue to push himself up all the time while coordinating his hands and feet.

It worked!

Jevon was so ecstatic that he didn't realize his mother had gone. He was now sitting on a limb with a big, luscious Julie mango right in front of him.

He lay himself on the limb like he'd seen the lizards do and crawled over to get the fruit.

The feeling was indescribable. It felt better than when he had first learned to ride his bicycle, even better than when he had first flown on the airplane.

No, this was different. This was a mystery solved!

It was a very high achievement— and to think his mother had the greatest clue he needed. So, he rewarded her with the mango.

For him the mango was not important now. In fact, he could pick as many mangos as he wished. He had not only learned how to climb, but he had also mastered the skill of climbing.

Mystery solved! And what an adventure it was!